'Once the

are aroused,
once they are
determined,
nothing on earth
and nothing in
heaven will make
women give way;
it is impossible.'

Material has been sourced from newspaper articles, pamphlets, posters and legal documents published between 1867 and 1928.

The Suffragettes

PENGUIN BOOKS

PENGUIN CLASSICS

UK | USA | Canada | Ireland | Australia
India | New Zealand | South Africa

Penguin Classics is part of the Penguin Random House group of companies whose addresses can be found at global.penguinrandomhouse.com.

This selection first published in Penguin Classics 2016
007

Set in 9.5/13 pt Baskerville 10 Pro
Printed in Great Britain by Clays Ltd, Elcograf S.p.A.

A CIP catalogue record for this book is available
from the British Library

ISBN: 978–0–241–25211–6

www.greenpenguin.co.uk

Contents

FOURTEEN REASONS FOR SUPPORTING WOMEN'S SUFFRAGE.

1. —Because it is the foundation of all political liberty that those who obey the Law should be able to have a voice in choosing those who make the Law.
2. —Because Parliament should be the reflection of the wishes of the people.
3. —Because Parliament cannot fully reflect the wishes of the people, when the wishes of women are without any direct representation.
4. —Because most Laws affect women as much as men, and some Laws affect women especially.
5. —Because the Laws which affect women especially are now passed without consulting those persons whom they are intended to benefit.
6. —Because Laws affecting children should be regarded from the woman's point of view as well as the man's.
7. —Because every session questions affecting the home come up for consideration in Parliament.
8. —Because women have experience which which should be helpfully brought to bear on domestic legislation.
9. —Because to deprive women of the vote is to lower their position in common estimation.
10. —Because the possession of the vote would increase the sense of responsibility amongst women towards questions of public importance.
11. —Because public-spirited mothers make public-spirited sons.
12. —Because large numbers of intelligent, thoughtful, hard-working women desire the franchise.
13. —Because the objections raised against their having the franchise are based on sentiment, not on reason.
14. —Because—to sum all reasons up in one—it is for the common good of all.

Printed by Bradbury, Agnew & Co., Ltd., London and Tonbridge, for the National Union of Women's Suffrage Societies, and Published by them at 25, Victoria Street, S.W.

SUFFRAGE

NUWSS

The National Union of Women's Suffrage Societies was formed in 1867 and united many smaller suffrage organizations. Under the leadership of Millicent Fawcett, the NUWSS's method was non-confrontational and constitutional.

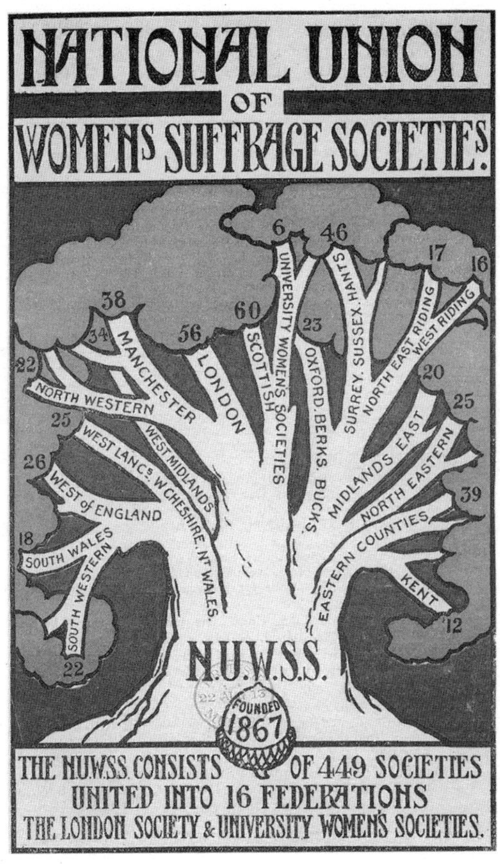

Front cover of leaflet produced by the NUWSS, 1913
(copyright © the British Library, London, UK/Bridgeman Images).

Read "The Common Cause." 1d. weekly.

January, 1914.

B 111. *Send for free Catalogue of N.U.W.S.S. publications*

National Union of Women's Suffrage Societies

14, GREAT SMITH STREET, WESTMINSTER, LONDON, S.W.

LAW-ABIDING. NON-PARTY.

President: Mrs. HENRY FAWCETT, LL.D.

Colours: Red, White and Green.

Votes for Mothers

THEY TELL YOU

"The Woman's Place is the Home."

Well, if you had **votes** you might have **better homes;** and if you had better homes your **children** would have **a better chance.**

You have seen many a poor woman's baby as fine and healthy at birth as the child of any wealthy woman in the land. You have seen that baby gradually pine, grow thin, pale, fretful, and at last sicken and die, in spite of all its mother's love and care.

Why did that Baby Die?

Most likely it died because the house into which it was born was unhealthy, insanitary, overcrowded, and consequently full of poisonous germs.

To prove this go to Birmingham. There you will find that, in a poor and crowded part of the city, of every **1,000** babies born **331** die. But, only 4½ miles away, in the garden village of Bournville where the people have good and healthy houses, of every **1,000** babies born only **65** die. That means that of every **five** babies who die in the unhealthy houses only **one** would have died, had it been born in a healthy home—four of the five dead babies **need not have died at all.** They were killed by conditions which ought not to exist—conditions which their mothers had no power to change.

That is why **mothers** want votes. For then they could send men to Parliament who would say: "We have had enough of this wholesale slaughter of innocent babies. We will insist on healthy homes for the people, so that the babies may live and thrive."

Mothers, **it could be done.** It **will** be done when you have power and **use** your power to send to Parliament, men who will talk less about women stopping at home and do more to see that women have decent homes to stop in. For the sake of the babies demand

Votes for Mothers.

4d. per 100, 2/6 per 1,000.

Published by the National Union of Women's Suffrage Societies,
14, Great Smith Street, Westminster; and
Printed by The Templar Printing Works, Edmund Street, Birmingham.

Published in the National Union of Women's Suffrage Societies newspaper (NUWSS) in July 1912.

PUBLISHER: NATIONAL UNION OF WOMEN'S SUFFRAGE SOCIETIES, 1913.

WHY WORKING WOMEN WANT THE VOTE

Some Reasons Why Working Women Want the Vote

Because as long as women cannot vote for Members of Parliament they are not asked what they want, and they are treated like children who do not know what is good or what is bad for them.

Because only those who wear the shoe know where it pinches, and women know best what they want and what they don't want.

Because Members of Parliament must attend to the wants and wishes of those who have votes, and they have not time to attend to the wants and wishes of women who have not got votes.

Because laws are made which specially affect women's work and the work of their children.

Because if women are working as dressmakers, tailoresses, printers, confectioners, and laundresses, or in any factory or workshop, the laws under which they work are made for women without women being asked if these laws are good or bad for them.

Because if the laws under which women work are bad, women cannot have those laws changed unless they have the vote.

Because the vote has been given to women in some of our Colonies and has been of great use.

Because the way to help women is to give them the means of helping themselves.

Because the vote is the best and most direct way by which women can get their wishes and wants attended to.

On July 26, 1913, 50,000 NUWSS supporters from all across Britain rallied in Hyde Park for the right to vote.

WSPU

The Women's Social and Political Union was founded in 1903 by Emmeline Pankhurst who was disillusioned with the constitutional methods of campaigning employed by the NUWSS. The WSPU preferred to raise public and media awareness of the campaign by militant action.

Poster advertising *The Suffragette* newspaper, 1912 (copyright © the Museum of London).

THE GIRL SUFFRAGIST.

"Brought up in Socialistic Beliefs."

When Dora Thewlis, aged seventeen, the little factory operative from Huddersfield who demonstrated outside the House of Commons last week with the other seventy arrested Suffragettes comes before the Westminster magistrate on Wednesday upon remand, Mr. Horace Smith will find, apparently, that his sympathy and indignation have been wasted.

The magistrate, it will be recalled, spoke to the girl in the dock whose shawl-covered head just appeared above the ledge, somewhat feelingly; "You are only a child; you ought to be in school. Will you go home again? I think it was perfectly disgraceful—and the circumstances reflect the gravest discredit on all concerned—bringing you up to London. I shall remand you for a week and write to your parents, and I hope I shall see them on Wednesday."

The magistrate seems to have written in due course to her mother a kindly and admonitory letter, pointing out the risks of London, and offering to send the girl home again on Wednesday, when her fare would be paid out of the poor box.

Indignation is the feeling aroused in the parents of Dora Thewlis by Mr. Horace Smith's communication.

"We have brought her up in Socialistic and Progressive beliefs," said the mother. "She and I were the first Huddersfield people to assist Mrs. Pankhurst in the recent by-election."

Mr. Thewlis said: "She has written asking me to ask the magistrate to give her the same sentence as the others have received." The father intends to comply with her wish.

The Times, 1907.

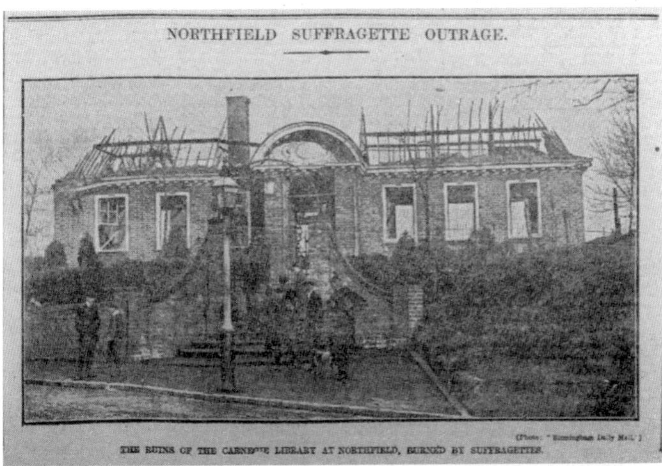

NORTHFIELD SUFFRAGETTE OUTRAGE.

(Photo: "Birmingham Daily Mail.")

THE RUINS OF THE CARNEGIE LIBRARY AT NORTHFIELD, BURNED BY SUFFRAGETTES.

Photograph (1914) of the damage caused by the suffragette action at Northfield Library. Local suffragettes set fire to the library at night, and the building and its contents were destroyed. A book by Christabel Pankhurst was left at the site, along with a note reading, 'To start your new library'.

HORRIBLE PAIN.

"On Sunday morning the religious service which is held for inmates of the infirmary was going on over my head, and their first hymn had just finished when the doctor and the wardresses appeared to feed me. I was violently sick during this feeding, but it was nothing to the time I had in the evening. When the tube was put up my nose it twisted, and part of it came out of my mouth. The pain was so horrible I felt as if my nose was being pulled off, and I struggled violently. At this the doctor said, 'After all, it is only an indiarubber tube,' but to me it felt more like a crowbar. I was violently sick, and when the operation was over I cried with relief and pain.

"The following morning they tried the throat tube, and the doctor gave me the choice of a gag. That night they gave me something rather thick, which took a long time to go through the tube, and made me feel very ill.

"On New Year's Day I had been sleeping so badly that they gave me a sleeping draught.

"The prison officials were most kind, and seemed to loathe the abominable practice of forcible feeding."

The Suffragette (extract), 1913.

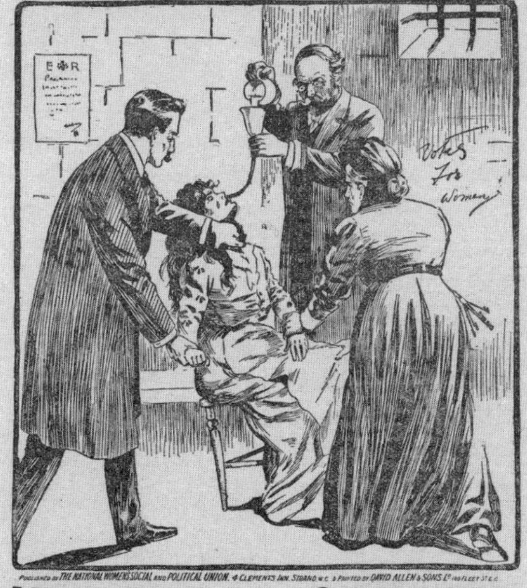

By-Election poster: 'Torturing Women in Prison', from *Votes for Women* newspaper, 1909.

WSPU poster.
The Prisoners (Temporary Discharge for Ill Health) Act 1913 (also known as the 'Cat and Mouse Act') was an Act of Parliament permitting suffragettes undertaking hunger strikes in prison to be released if they became ill. However, the Act allowed for the re-imprisonment of the hunger strikers upon their recovery on their original charges. The nickname of the Act refers to a cat playing with its prey before finishing it off.

LETTER WRITTEN BY EMMELINE PANKHURST
TO MEMBERS OF WPSU, JANUARY 10, 1913.

VOTES FOR WOMEN
The Women's Social and Political Union

MRS. PANKHURST, *Hon. Treasurer*
OFFICE: LINCOLN'S INN HOUSE, KINGSWAY, W.C.
MRS. MABEL TUKE, *Hon. Sec.*

All communications, Auditors: MESSRS. SAYERS & WESSON
unless marked 'private' will be opened

Chartered Accountants, 19. Hanover Square, W.
by the Hon. Secretary Telegraphic Address–WOSPOLU, LONDON
Telephone 2724 Holborn (three lines)

January 10th, 1913
Private and Confidential

Dear Friend,
The Prime Minister has announced that in the week beginning January 20th the Women's Amendments to the Manhood Suffrage Bill will be discussed and voted upon.

This means that within a few short days the fate of these Amendments will be finally decided.

The W.S.P.U. has from the first declined to call any truce on the strength of the Prime Minister's so-called pledge, and has refused to depend upon the Amendments in question, because the Government have not accepted the responsibility of getting them carried. There are, however, some Suffragists–and there may be some even in the ranks of the W.S.P.U.–who hope against hope that in spite of the Government's intrigues an unofficial Amendment may be carried. Feeling as they do, these Suffragists are tempted to hold their hand as far as militancy is concerned, until after the fate of the Amendments is known.

But every member of the W.S.P.U. recognises that the defeat of the Amendments will make militancy more a moral duty and more a political necessity than it has ever been before. We must prepare beforehand to deal with that situation!

There are degrees of militancy. Some women are able to go further than others in militant action and each woman is the judge of her own duty so far as that is concerned. To be militant in some way or other is, however, a moral obligation. It is a duty which every woman will owe to her own conscience and self-respect, to other women who are less fortunate than she herself is, and to all those who are to come after her.

If any woman refrains from militant protest against the

injury done by the Government and the House of Commons to women and to the race, she will share the responsibility for the crime. Submission under such circumstances will be itself a crime.

I know that the defeat of the Amendments will prove to thousands of women that to rely only on peaceful, patient methods, is to court failure, and that militancy is inevitable.

We must, as I have said, prepare to meet the crisis before it arises. Will you therefore tell me (by letter, if it is not possible to do so by word of mouth), that you are ready to take your share in manifesting in a practical manner your indignation at the betrayal of our cause.

Yours sincerely,
(Signed) E. Pankhurst

DAILY SKETCH.

THURSDAY, JUNE 5, 1913. (Registered as a Newspaper.) ONE HALFPENNY.

HISTORY'S MOST WONDERFUL DERBY: FIRST HORSE DISQUALIFIED: A 100 TO 1 CHANCE WINS: SUFFRAGETTE NEARLY KILLED BY THE KING'S COLT.

Miss Emily Davison. The woman falling to the ground. The King's horse, Anmer, falls on his jockey. Herbert Jones.

Yesterday's Derby was extraordinary. Not only was Craganour, the favourite, disqualified after finishing first, the race being awarded to Aboyeur; a suffragette ran across the course at Tattenham Corner and seized the bridle of the King's horse. The King's horse and jockey were thrown to the ground, while the woman was nearly killed. The extraordinary photograph seen above was taken by the *Daily Sketch* a second after the horse and the woman fell to the ground.

The Daily Sketch front cover, June 1913.

The Adventures of the Woman Who Did It.
MISS DAVISON'S CAREER.
Always in the Battle Line of the Militants.

Miss Davison is one of the most noted women in the suffragist movement. She is a militant of militants, and has certainly earned for herself the description one of the officials at the W.S.P.U. offices gave the *Daily Sketch* yesterday: "A woman who fears nothing; permanent address Holloway Prison."

The daughter of Charles Edward and Margaret Davison, she was born at Blackheath.

She graduated B.A. with honours at London University.

Joining the W.S.P.U. in November, 1906, she soon became one of the most prominent of its members.

Here is a list of her offences and imprisonments, which began in March, 1909:—

March 30, 1909.—One month for an offence while on a deputation.

July 30.—Two months for obstruction at Limehouse, released after five and a half days' hunger strike.

September 4.—Stone-throwing at White City, Manchester, two months, but released after two and a half days' hunger strike.

October 20.—Stone-throwing at Radcliffe, one month's hard labour on each count; hunger struck, forcibly fed, defied prison authorities, who turned hose-pipe on her. Afterwards she brought an action against visiting magistrates of Strangeways Prison and won her case.

December 14, 1911.—Arrested for setting fire to pillar-boxes in London, sentenced to six months' imprisonment, hunger struck twice, and released ten days before expiration of sentence on account of injuries received while being forcibly fed.

November 30, 1912.—Ten days' imprisonment at Aberdeen for assaulting Baptist minister whom she said she mistook for Mr. Lloyd George. Released after four days after hunger-striking for that period.

Among her other exploits are:—

Hid in hot-air shaft of House of Commons.

Hid in crypt in House of Commons twice.

Miss Davison is a member of the Kilburn branch of the W.S.P.U., but she is a guerilla fighter, and as a rule the officers of the movement had no knowledge of what she intended to do.

According to one of the women at the head offices this was the case in the Derby incident.

"She is a level-headed woman," said the official to the *Daily Sketch,* "and when she threw herself at the horse she would realise fully that she was practically throwing her life away. You may take it from me that if she made her mind up to do anything, the fear of death would not cause her to hesitate for a single moment."

Accompanying biography from *The Daily Sketch*. (She later died from her injuries.)

'Freedom or Death' speech by Emmeline Pankhurst

DELIVERED AT HARTFORD, CONNECTICUT – 13TH NOVEMBER, 1913.

I do not come here as an advocate, because whatever position the suffrage movement may occupy in the United States of America, in England it has passed beyond the realm of advocacy and it has entered into the sphere of practical politics. It has become the subject of revolution and civil war, and so tonight I am not here to advocate woman suffrage. American suffragists can do that very well for themselves.

I am here as a soldier who has temporarily left the field of battle in order to explain – it seems strange it should have to be explained – what civil war is like when civil war is waged by women. I am not only here as a soldier temporarily absent from the field at battle; I am here – and that, I think, is the strangest part of my coming – I am here as a person who, according to the law courts of my country, it has been decided, is of no value to the community at all; and I am adjudged because of my life to be a dangerous person, under sentence of penal servitude in a convict prison.

It is not at all difficult if revolutionaries come to you

from Russia, if they come to you from China, or from any other part of the world, if they are men. But since I am a woman it is necessary to explain why women have adopted revolutionary methods in order to win the rights of citizenship. We women, in trying to make our case clear, always have to make as part of our argument, and urge upon men in our audience the fact – a very simple fact – that women are human beings.

Suppose the men of Hartford had a grievance, and they laid that grievance before their legislature, and the legislature obstinately refused to listen to them, or to remove their grievance, what would be the proper and the constitutional and the practical way of getting their grievance removed? Well, it is perfectly obvious at the next general election the men of Hartford would turn out that legislature and elect a new one.

But let the men of Hartford imagine that they were not in the position of being voters at all, that they were governed without their consent being obtained, that the legislature turned an absolutely deaf ear to their demands, what would the men of Hartford do then? They couldn't vote the legislature out. They would have to choose; they would have to make a choice of two evils: they would either have to submit indefinitely to an unjust state of affairs, or they would have to rise up and adopt some of the antiquated means by which men in the past got their grievances remedied.

Your forefathers decided that they must have

representation for taxation, many, many years ago. When they felt they couldn't wait any longer, when they laid all the arguments before an obstinate British government that they could think of, and when their arguments were absolutely disregarded, when every other means had failed, they began by the tea party at Boston, and they went on until they had won the independence of the United States of America.

It is about eight years since the word militant was first used to describe what we were doing. It was not militant at all, except that it provoked militancy on the part of those who were opposed to it. When women asked questions in political meetings and failed to get answers, they were not doing anything militant. In Great Britain it is a custom, a time-honoured one, to ask questions of candidates for parliament and ask questions of members of the government. No man was ever put out of a public meeting for asking a question. The first people who were put out of a political meeting for asking questions, were women; they were brutally ill-used; they found themselves in jail before 24 hours had expired.

We were called militant, and we were quite willing to accept the name. We were determined to press this question of the enfranchisement of women to the point where we were no longer to be ignored by the politicians.

You have two babies very hungry and wanting to be fed. One baby is a patient baby, and waits indefinitely until its mother is ready to feed it.

The other baby is an impatient baby and cries lustily, screams and kicks and makes everybody unpleasant until it is fed. Well, we know perfectly well which baby is attended to first. That is the whole history of politics. You have to make more noise than anybody else, you have to make yourself more obtrusive than anybody else, you have to fill all the papers more than anybody else, in fact you have to be there all the time and see that they do not snow you under.

When you have warfare things happen; people suffer; the noncombatants suffer as well as the combatants. And so it happens in civil war. When your forefathers threw the tea into Boston Harbour, a good many women had to go without their tea. It has always seemed to me an extraordinary thing that you did not follow it up by throwing the whiskey overboard; you sacrificed the women; and there is a good deal of warfare for which men take a great deal of glorification which has involved more practical sacrifice on women than it has on any man. It always has been so. The grievances of those who have got power, the influence of those who have got power commands a great deal of attention; but the wrongs and the grievances of those people who have no power at all are apt to be absolutely ignored. That is the history of humanity right from the beginning.

Well, in our civil war people have suffered, but you cannot make omelettes without breaking eggs; you cannot have civil war without damage to something. The great thing is to see that no more damage is done than is absolutely necessary, that you do just as much as will arouse enough feeling to bring about peace, to bring about an honourable peace for the combatants; and that is what we have been doing.

We entirely prevented stockbrokers in London from telegraphing to stockbrokers in Glasgow and vice versa: for one whole day telegraphic communication was entirely stopped. I am not going to tell you how it was done. I am not going to tell you how the women got to the mains and cut the wires; but it was done.

It was done, and it was proved to the authorities that weak women, suffrage women, as we are supposed to be, had enough ingenuity to create a situation of that kind. Now, I ask you, if women can do that, is there any limit to what we can do except the limit we put upon ourselves?

If you are dealing with an industrial revolution, if you get the men and women of one class rising up against the men and women of another class, you can locate the difficulty; if there is a great industrial strike, you know exactly where the violence is and how the warfare is going to be waged; but in our war against the government you can't locate it. We wear no mark; we belong to every class; we permeate every class of the community from the highest to the lowest; and so you see in the woman's civil war the dear men of my country are discovering it is absolutely impossible to deal with it: you cannot locate it, and you cannot stop it.

'Put them in prison,' they said, 'that will stop it.' But it didn't stop it at all: instead of the women giving it up, more women did it, and more and more and more women did it until there were 300 women at a time, who had not broken a single law, only 'made a nuisance of themselves' as the politicians say.

Then they began to legislate. The British government has passed more stringent laws to deal with this agitation than it ever found necessary during all the history of political agitation in my country. They were able to deal with the revolutionaries of the Chartists' time; they were able to deal with the trades union agitation; they were able to deal with the revolutionaries later on when the Reform Acts were passed: but the ordinary law has not sufficed to curb insurgent women. They had to dip back into the middle ages to find a means of repressing the women in revolt.

They have said to us, government rests upon force, the women haven't force, so they must submit.

Well, we are showing them that government does not rest upon force at all: it rests upon consent. As long as women consent to be unjustly governed, they can be, but directly women say: 'We withhold our consent, we will not be governed any longer so long as that government is unjust.' Not by the forces of civil war can you govern the very weakest woman. You can kill that woman, but she escapes you then; you cannot govern her. No power on earth can govern a human being, however feeble, who withholds his or her consent.

When they put us in prison at first, simply for taking petitions, we submitted; we allowed them to dress us in prison clothes; we allowed them to put us in solitary confinement; we allowed them to put us amongst the most degraded of criminals; we learned of some of the appalling evils of our so-called civilisation that we could not have learned in any other way. It was valuable experience, and we were glad to get it.

I have seen men smile when they heard the words 'hunger strike', and yet I think there are very few men today who would be prepared to adopt a 'hunger strike' for any cause. It is only people who feel an intolerable sense of oppression who would adopt a means of that kind. It means you refuse food until you are at death's door, and then the authorities have to choose between letting you die, and letting you go; and then they let the women go.

Now, that went on so long that the government felt that they were unable to cope. It was [then] that, to the shame of the British government, they set the example to authorities all over the world of feeding sane, resisting human beings by force. There may be doctors in this meeting: if so, they know it is one thing to feed by force an insane person; but it is quite another thing to feed a sane, resisting human being who resists with every nerve and with every fibre of her body the indignity and the outrage of forcible feeding.

Now, that was done in England, and the government thought they had crushed us. But they found that it did not quell the agitation, that more and more women came in and even passed that terrible ordeal, and they were obliged to let them go.

Then came the legislation – the 'Cat and Mouse Act'. The home secretary said: 'Give me the power to let these women go when they are at death's door, and leave them at liberty under license until they have recovered their health again and then bring them back.' It was passed to repress the agitation, to make the women yield – because that is what it has really come to, ladies and gentlemen. It has come to a battle between the women and the government as to who shall yield first, whether they will yield and give us the vote, or whether we will give up our agitation.

Well, they little know what women are. Women are very slow to rouse, but once they are aroused, once they are determined, nothing on earth and nothing in heaven will make women give way; it is impossible. And so this 'Cat and Mouse Act' which is being used against women today has failed. There are women lying at death's door, recovering enough strength to undergo operations who have not given in and won't give in, and who will be prepared, as soon as they get up from their sick beds, to go on as before. There are women who are being carried from their sick beds on stretchers into meetings. They are too weak to speak, but they go amongst their fellow workers just to show that their spirits are unquenched, and that their spirit is alive, and they mean to go on as long as life lasts.

Now, I want to say to you who think women cannot succeed, we have brought the government of England to this position, that it has to face this alternative: either women are to be killed or women are to have the vote.

I ask American men in this meeting, what would you say if in your state you were faced with that alternative, that you must either kill them or give them their citizenship? Well, there is only one answer to that alternative, there is only one way out – you must give those women the vote.

You won your freedom in America when you had the revolution, by bloodshed, by sacrificing human life. You won the civil war by the sacrifice of human life when you decided to emancipate the negro. You have left it to women in your land, the men of all civilised countries have left it to women, to work out their own salvation. That is the way in which we women of England are doing. Human life for us is sacred, but we say if any life is to be sacrificed it shall be ours; we won't do it ourselves, but we will put the enemy in the position where they will have to choose between giving us freedom or giving us death.

So here am I. I come in the intervals of prison appearance. I come after having been four times imprisoned under the 'Cat and Mouse Act', probably going back to be rearrested as soon as I set my foot on British soil. I come to ask you to help to win this fight. If we win it, this hardest of all fights, then, to be sure, in the future it is going to be made easier for women all over the world to win their fight when their time comes.

The Suffragettes defaced the penny coin, ensuring their core message was distributed as widely as possible for years. Because of the low monetary value of a copper, the banks decided not to recall it from circulation (copyright © the Trustees of the British Museum. All rights reserved.).

ANTI-SUFFRAGE

Women's National Anti-Suffrage League Manifesto

(a) Because the spheres of men and women, owing to natural causes, are essentially different, and therefore their share in the public management of the State should be different.

(b) Because the complex modern State depends for its very existence on naval and military power, diplomacy, finance, and the great mining, constructive, shipping and transport industries, in none of which can women take any practical part. Yet it is upon these matters, and the vast interests involved in them, that the work of Parliament largely turns.

(c) Because by the concession of the local government vote and the admission of women to County and Borough Councils, the nation has opened a wide sphere of public work and influence to women, which is within their powers. To make proper use of it, however, will tax all the energies that women have to spare, apart from the care of the home and the development of the individual life.

(d) Because the influence of women in social causes will be diminished rather than increased by the possession of the Parliamentary vote. At present they stand, in matters of social reform, apart from and beyond party politics, and are listened to accordingly. The legitimate influence of women in politics – in all classes, rich and poor – will always be in proportion to their education and common sense. But the deciding power of the Parliamentary vote should be left to men, whose physical force is ultimately responsible for the conduct of the State.

(e) Because all the reforms which are put forward as reasons for the vote can be obtained by other means than the vote, as is proved by the general history of the laws relating to women and children during the past century. The channels of public opinion are always freely open to women. Moreover, the services which women can with advantage render to the nation in the field of social and educational reform, and in the investigation of social problems, have been recognised by Parliament. Women have been included in Royal Commissions, and admitted to a share in local government. The true path of progress seems to lie in farther development along these lines. Representative women, for instance, might be brought into closer consultative relation with Government departments, in matters where the special interests of women are concerned.

(f) Because any measure for the enfranchisement of women must either (1) concede the vote to women on the same terms as to men, and thereby in practice involve an unjust and invidious limitation; or (2) by giving the vote to wives of voters tend to the introduction of political differences into domestic life; or (3) by the adoption of adult suffrage, which seems the inevitable result of admitting the principle, place the female vote in an overpowering majority.

(g) Because, finally, the danger which might arise from the concession of woman-suffrage, in the case of a State burdened with such complex and far-reaching responsibilities as England, is out of all proportion to the risk run by those smaller communities which have adopted it. The admission to full political power of a number of voters debarred by nature and circumstances from the average political knowledge and experience open to men, would weaken the central governing forces of the State, and be fraught with peril to the country.

'Mummy's a Suffragette' anti-suffrage postcard, 1909.
A poem on the back reads:
'Mummy is a Suffragette
And I am no one's pet
Oh! Why am I left all alone
To cry and suffer yet.'

(copyright © the Museum of London)

Punch: 'The Dignity of the Franchise', 1905 (copyright © the British Library, London, UK/Bridgeman Images).

"VOTES FOR WOMEN," NEVER!

Men of England, your interests and those of your families, and the welfare of the country are in danger. Rally to prevent it.

A large number of women are demanding votes for Parliament. A large number of amiable but short-sighted **M.P.'s are willing to grant the demand, without getting your permission.**

Remember there are **1,300,000 more women than men in the United Kingdom,** and if everybody has a vote, men will be outnumbered, **women will have the dominant political power**—in fact, the Government of the Country and the Empire will have passed from your hands to those of women.

Resent this attempted **tyranny** and let the Suffragists know that you simply will not have **petticoat government** for this old Country and world-wide Empire.

They call it "justice" and "equality." It is nothing of the kind. It is the **subjection of man to woman,** turning the order of nature upside down. It is contrary to commonsense, to experience, and to history. Men in all ages have had to do the brunt of the world's business, and ought to govern.

Don't make yourselves and your country the **laughing stock of the world,** but keep political power where it ought to be—in the hands of men.

Above all, let your M.P. know what you think, and tell him **not to vote** for this infamous injustice and topsy turvey proposal till he knows through the ballot box what his constituents wish about it.

Play up and save your country. Save suffragist women from themselves, and other women from Suffragists.

Help the good work of defence by joining the
NATIONAL LEAGUE FOR OPPOSING WOMAN SUFFRAGE,
Caxton House, Tothill Street, S.W.

Funds urgently needed to extend the Campaign.

Printed by the National Press Agency Limited, Whitefriars House, Carmelite Street, E.C., and Published by The National League for Opposing Woman Suffrage, Caxton House, Tothill Street, Westminster, S.W.

Price 3s. 6d. per 1000.

'"Votes for Women," Never!' Anti-Suffragette handbill from the National League for Opposing Woman Suffrage.

THE OPPONENTS' VIEW. WOMEN'S NATIONAL ANTI-SUFFRAGE LEAGUE.

BY MRS FREDERIC HARRISON.

The invitation to our league to set forth our views in the *Queen* comes at an opportune moment, and is in great contrast with the illiberality of many journals, who do their best to close their columns against us. We often hear of the injustice done to that small minority of women who demand the Parliamentary vote; we do not hear of the injustice done to that large majority of women who have conscientious objections to the vote, and feel that in every scheme of franchise as yet set forth a great wrong is intended to the wives and mothers of this country.

The public has hardly had time or opportunity as yet to understand our position. This franchise movement for women is too recent a growth to have become a practical question, and the women who disapproved it, did not feel it their business to oppose or to thwart those other women who sought to convince them and the general public. It is always a painful and an unpleasant task for women to oppose other women who command respect, even though their arguments may not carry conviction.

The constitutional ladies, as I may call them, for they

made their demands in a constitutional way, have been swept out of sight by a number of "irresponsibles," who have. as we think, brought discredit on the cause, and forced us into action. Their appearance on the scene entirely changed the situation, which Mr Asquith's guarded pronouncement has made acute. The women who did not want the vote were forced into a position of defence, and had to seek some way of putting their case before politicians and the country. Our silence would have implied consent and approval.

As I hope to write with respect and consideration for our opponents, I must say a word in justification of the term "irresponsible." The somewhat rough gambols of the militant ladies have not, as we think, done much harm, beyond annoying candidates for Parliament, who, as the old Italian vetturino used to say, "sont là pour cela." The cleverness and energy of these ladies is beyond dispute; so is the fertility of their imagination, though they do not bear imprisonment with the quiet dignity of the passive resisters. But we agree that prison is not a pleasant place.

How, then, do I justify the term irresponsible? I will quote from a well-known Socialist organ, presumably a friend to the cause of woman's suffrage:

> Listening to Miss Christabel Pankhurst the other day . . . If the limited suffrage for women were passed into law, that is to say, all the disabilities under which women suffer—physical, mental, economic, social: and moral—would all be done away with at a stroke. It is the lack of the vote, so

> we were given to understand. that renders women liable to sweating, that subjects them to bad husbands, that drives them into prostitution, that cripples their intelligence, &c. . . . We admire the energy and self-sacrifice the suffragettes have shown in a poor cause. But their misrepresentations will finally wreck them.

The suffragette's millennium is a dream; but though it is well that our young women should dream dreams and see visions of a happier future, it is not well that they should make promises which cannot be made good, or that they should talk irresponsible "rubbish" (I quote again) to poor working women.

We have waited long for some word or sign from the constitutional suffragists to curb and restrain this flood of frothy effervescence. They have amongst them women of distinction well able to prick these economic and other bubbles, but no word or sign has come. So it is that the women of our league find a duty thrust upon them to speak plainly their mind, and to say openly what they think of a movement which seems to them morbid and retrograde.

We consider that the extension of the suffrage to another sex is no simple addition to the roll of electors; it is not analogous to an extension of the male franchise. It is a vast upheaval of social institutions and habits, which must cut into the peace and well-being of families and re-act for harm on the education of children.

We quote from our leaflet "Woman's Suffrage—and After!":

> Let it not be supposed that this agitation will be appeased by small concessions of a limited suffrage. If it be given exclusively to spinsters it will be an offence to wives and mothers who are certainly not less qualified to vote on national issues. If it be given to wives it will divide homes and leave decisions to the sex which cannot defend the State nor enforce obedience to the laws. If it be extended to all adults it threatens us with a majority of women voters.

These difficulties have never been met or answered, nor has any suffragist lady told us how she proposes to avoid inflicting a gross injustice on the bulk of Englishwomen. The vote, of course, first; but after will come the demand to be admitted to Parliament, to sit on juries, to be judges of the land, &c. These things are not written fair on any one charter of reforms, but the suffragists intend to have them all. We women of the league would impose no artificial restrictions upon our sex as to the work they should do, nor would we erect barriers in the way of their highest development on their own lines. But we see very clearly that a vast amount of the most important work of the world is waiting for woman to do. If we may credit so close an observer as George Gissing, we see that women are failing in their own special work. We think that the vote is but the prelude to a social revolution which must set back progress, for we believe in the division of functions as the keystone of civilisation. It is as if the animals on a farm should insist on changing places—the cows insist upon drawing the coach, while the horses strive in vain to chew the cud and ruminate.

There are two very serious matters which must engage the attention of Parliament for a generation. The question of the national defence is only less pressing than the question of finance. Both are bound up closely together, and linked to them is that other question of Poor Law reform and old age pensions. What have women to contribute to the serious problem of the national defence? What to that other equally serious problem of the national finance? Men in these matters are entirely responsible; would it not be as unjust as unwise to hamper their action with woman's interference? The opinion of women on the Poor Law and old age pensions, on the other hand, is an important factor, and is being heard and weighed all up and down the country already.

It is sometimes said that the women who are on our side know nothing personally of the hard work of the world, and are but trying mischievously to keep other women from their own. If it were so we should fail, and deserve to fail. We find our greatest support amongst these very women workers. Our supporters come from all classes, rich and poor, in town and country, from all degrees of workers. We have eminent scientific women, writers, journalists, nurses, teachers in high schools, in board schools, many literary women, farmers' wives and daughters, labourers' wives, washerwomen, domestic servants, old and young, with workers in factories in London and other great cities. These all make up a huge army of intelligent women all eager against the vote.

The suffragist camp suffers probably, as we do, from a certain number of women who cannot be stirred out of their indifference. Let us trust that this conflict over the suffrage question will at last rouse them. For we consider it a very important question, and we shall be glad to hear from all your readers who would like to know more of our doings, or who sympathise with us. Our indefatigable secretaries are always glad to answer questions, and will send literature on application with instructions how to join our society and how best to help us. Our headquarters are Caxton House, Tothill-street, Westminster; branches of the league are being formed up and down the country.

E. B. HARRISON.

Our picture is of the badge given to members of the Women's National Anti-Suffrage League, which has been formed for the purpose of combating the Votes for Women movement. The league is under the presidency of Mrs Humphry Ward, and among its distinguished members may be mentioned Lord James of Hereford, Earl of Shaftesbury, Lord Harrogate, Lady Wantage, Lady Roberts, Lady Haliburton, and the Countess of Coventry, and very many men and women well-known in the world of literature and social work.

'The Opponents' View: Women's National Anti-Suffrage League.'
From *The Queen*, September 26, 1908.

VICTORY

EXTRACT OF LADY ASTOR'S MAIDEN SPEECH IN THE HOUSE OF COMMONS

24 February 1920

Viscountess ASTOR: I shall not begin by craving the indulgence of the House. I am only too conscious of the indulgence and the courtesy of the House. I know that it was very difficult for some hon. Members to receive the first lady M.P. into the House. [HON. MEMBERS: "Not at all!"] It was almost as difficult for some of them as it was for the lady M.P. herself to come in. Hon. Members, however, should not be frightened of what Plymouth sends out into the world. After all, I suppose when Drake and Raleigh wanted to set out on their venturesome careers, some cautious person said, "Do not do it; it has never been tried before. You stay at home, my sons, cruising around in home waters." I have no doubt that the same thing occurred when the Pilgrim Fathers set out. I have no doubt that there were cautious Christian brethren who did not understand their going into the wide seas to worship God in their own way. But, on the whole, the world is all the better for those venturesome and courageous west country people, and I would like to say that I am quite certain that the women of the whole world will not forget that it was the fighting men of Devon who dared to send the first woman to represent women in the Mother of Parliaments.

Now, as the west country people are a courageous lot, it is only right that one of their representatives should show some courage, and I am perfectly aware that it does take a bit of courage to address the House on that vexed question, Drink . . .

Do we want the welfare of the community, or do we want the prosperity of the Trade? Do we want national efficiency, or do we want national inefficiency? That is what it comes to. So I hope to be able to persuade the House. Are we really trying for a better world, or are we going to slip back to the same old world before 1914? I think that the hon. Member is not moving with the times . . .

He talks about the restrictions. I maintain that they brought a great deal of good to the community. There were two gains. First, there were the moral gains. I should like to tell you about them. The convictions of drunkenness among women during the War were reduced to one-fifth after these vexatious restrictions were brought in. I take women, because, as the hon. Member has said, most of the men were away fighting . . .

I do not think the country is really ripe for prohibition, but I am certain it is ripe for drastic drink reforms. [HON.

MEMBERS: "No!"] I know what I am talking about, and you must remember that women have got a vote now and we mean to use it, and use it wisely, not for the benefit of any section of society, but for the benefit of the whole. I want to see what the Government is going to do . . .

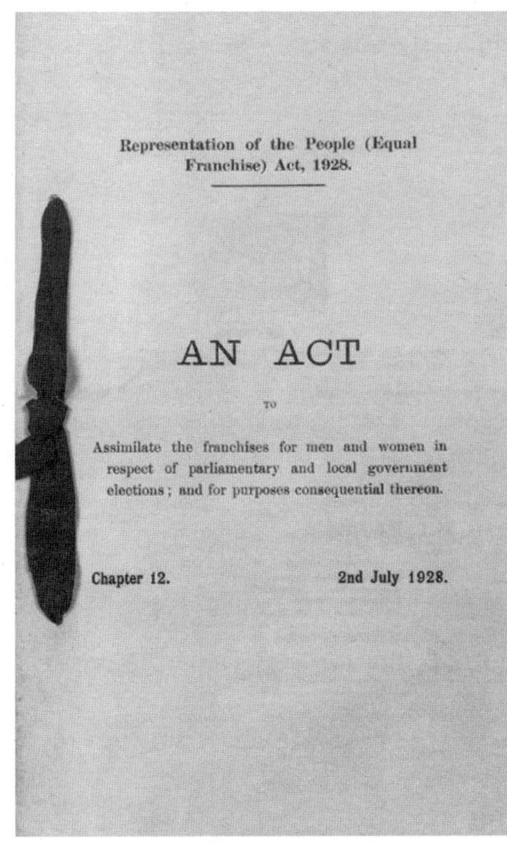

Representation of the People (Equal Franchise) Act, 1928.

AN ACT

TO

Assimilate the franchises for men and women in respect of parliamentary and local government elections; and for purposes consequential thereon.

Chapter 12. 2nd July 1928.

Representation of the People (Equal Franchise) Act, July 2, 1928. Gave the vote to both men and women over the age of 21, regardless of property ownership. Women became the majority of the electorate.

REPRESENTATION OF THE PEOPLE ACT, 1918

AN ACT
TO

Amend the Law with respect to Parliamentary and Local Government Franchises, and the Registration of Parliamentary and Local Government Electors, and the conduct of elections, and to provide for the Redistribution of Seats at Parliamentary Elections, and for other purposes connected therewith.

Chapter 64. 6th February 1918.

4.(1) A woman shall be entitled to be registered as a parliamentary elector for a constituency (other than a university constituency) if she – (a) has attained the age of thirty years; and (b) is not subject to any legal incapacity; and (c) is entitled to be registered as a local government elector in respect of the occupation in that constituency of land or premises (not being a dwelling-house) of a yearly value of not less than five pounds or of a dwelling-house, or is the wife of a husband entitled to be so registered.

(2) A woman shall be entitled to be registered as

parliamentary elector for a university constituency if she has attained the age of thirty years and either would be entitled to be so registered if she were a man, or has been admitted to and passed the final examination, and kept under the conditions required of women by the university the period of residence, necessary for a man to obtain a degree at any university forming, or forming part of, a university constituency which did not at the time the examination was passed admit women to degrees.

(3) A woman shall be entitled to be registered as a local government elector for any local government electoral area–

(a) where she would be entitled to be so registered if she were a man; and

(b) where she is the wife of a man who is entitled to be so registered in respect of premises in which they both reside, and she has attained the age of thirty years and is not subject to any legal incapacity.

For the purpose of this provision, a naval or military voter who is registered in respect of a residence qualification which he would have had but for his service, shall be deemed to be resident in accordance with the qualification.

Representation of People Act, 1918. Women over the age of 30 with the appropriate property qualifications were granted the right to vote.

[18 & 19 Geo. 5.] *REPRESENTATION OF THE PEOPLE (EQUAL FRANCHISE) ACT*, 1928. [Ch. 12.]

Chapter 12

An Act to assimilate the franchises for men and women in respect of parliamentary and local government elections; and for purposes consequential thereon. [2nd July 1928.]

Be it enacted by the King's most Excellent Majesty, by and with the advice and consent of the Lords Spiritual and Temporal, and Commons, in this present Parliament assembled, and by the authority of the same, as follows:—

1. For the purpose of providing that the parliamentary franchise shall be the same for men and women, subsections (1) and (2) of section four of the Representation of the People Act, 1918 (in this Act referred to as "the principal Act") shall be repealed and the following sections shall be substituted for sections one and two of that Act:—

(*Section to be substituted for the said section one.*)

" .—(1) A person shall be entitled to be registered as a parliamentary elector for a constituency (other than a university constituency), if he or she is of full age and not subject to any legal incapacity; and

(*a*) has the requisite residence qualification; or
(*b*) has the requisite business premises qualification; or
(*c*) is the husband or wife of a person entitled to be so registered in respect of a business premises qualification.

(2) A person, in order to have the requisite residence qualification or business premises qualification for a constituency—

(*a*) must on the last day of the qualifying period be residing in premises in the constituency, or occupying business premises in the constituency, as the case may be; and
(*b*) must during the whole of the qualifying period have resided in premises, or occupied business premises, as the case may be, in the constituency, or in another constituency within the same parliamentary borough or parliamentary county, or within a parliamentary borough or parliamentary county contiguous to that borough or county, or separated from that borough or county by water, not exceeding at the nearest point six miles in breadth, measured in the case of tidal water from low-water mark.

For the purposes of this subsection the administrative county of London shall be treated as a parliamentary borough.

(3) The expression 'business premises' in this section means land or other premises of the yearly value of not less than ten pounds occupied for the purpose of the business, profession, or trade of the person to be registered."

> (*Section to be substituted for the said section two.*)
>
> " . A person shall be entitled to be registered as a parliamentary elector for a university constituency if he or she is of full age and not subject to any legal incapacity, and has received a degree (other than an honorary degree) at any university forming, or forming part of, the constituency, or in the case of the Scottish universities is qualified under section twenty-seven of the Representation of the People (Scotland) Act, 1868, or if a woman, has been admitted to and passed the final examination, and kept under the conditions required of women by the university, the period of residence, necessary for a man to obtain a degree at any university forming, or forming part of, a university constituency which did not at the time the examination was passed admit women to degrees."

2. For the purpose of providing that the local government franchise shall be the same for men and women, subsection (3) of section four of the principal Act shall be repealed, and the following section shall be substituted for section three of that Act:

   " . A person shall be entitled to be registered as a local government elector for a local government electoral area if he or she is of full age and not subject to any legal incapacity, and—

(*a*) is on the last day of the qualifying period occupying as owner or tenant any land or premises in that area; and

(*b*) has during the whole of the qualifying period so occupied any land or premises in that area, or, if that area is not an administrative county or a county borough, in any administrative county or county borough in which the area is wholly or partly situate; or

(*c*) is the husband or wife of a person entitled to be so registered in respect of premises in which both the person so entitled and the husband or wife, as the case may be, reside:

Provided that—

(i) for the purposes of this section a person who inhabits any dwelling-house by virtue of any office, service, or employment, shall, if the dwelling-house is not inhabited by the person in whose service he or she is in such office, service, or employment, be deemed to occupy the dwelling-house as a tenant; and

(ii) for the purposes of this section the word tenant shall include a person who

FRANCHISE BILL TO-DAY.

5,240,000 MORE VOTERS.

COST OF TELEGRAMS.

(*From Our Parliamentary Correspondent.*)

In some ways the outstanding event of the week in Parliament will be the formal presentation of the Franchise Bill by Sir William Joynson-Hicks, the Home Secretary, this afternoon. No discussion is possible at this stage, but the Bill cannot be printed and circulated until it has been formally read a first time.

The official title of the measure is a Bill

> to amend the franchises for men and women in respect of Parliamentary and local government elections; and for purposes consequential thereon.

Its object is to ensure that in future men and women shall vote on equal terms. At one time it was thought that the Bill might be made highly controversial by the inclusion of a provision for the disqualification of electors who have been in receipt of poor relief. Wiser counsels have prevailed, however, and it is not expected that the Bill will give rise to much controversy. A section of the Conservative members may endeavour to secure an amendment to confer the franchise on women at 25 instead of at 21, but there is no prospect whatever of such an alteration being agreed to.

26,750,000 VOTERS.

It is estimated that as a result of the new Bill the electorate at the next General Election will consist of 12,250,000 men and 14,500,000 women—a total of 26,750,000. Before the Reform Act of 1832 the electorate numbered 435,391, and that measure added 217,386 voters to the register. The Act of 1867 added 938,427 names to the existing electorate of 1,056,659. In 1884 the Registration of the People Act added a further 1,762,087 names, and in 1918, when women of 30 were first given the vote, 13,000,000 new voters were added. Under the new Bill 5,240,000 women will be enfranchised. According to official estimates 1,590,000 will be under 25 years of age; 1,700,000 will be over 25 and under 30, and 1,950,000 will be women over 30 who are not now on the register. About 415,000 of the new electors will be women between the ages of 21 and 22—an average of about 700 in each constituency.

The business for consideration to-day in the House of Commons is the Air Estimates. After Sir Samuel Hoare has explained their salient features there will be a discussion on a Labour resolution to be moved by Mr. Barnes regretting that the Government did not advocate bolder proposals for aerial disarmament at the meeting of the Preparatory Commission at Geneva. At question time Sir Robert Lynn and Mr. Otho Nicholson will suggest to the Prime Minister that the report of the Hardman Lever Committee on the Inland Telegraph

Service should be submitted to the Imperial Wireless and Cables Conference, but there are other members who feel that the first duty of the Government is to make the report public. It has been in the possession of the Postmaster-General for some weeks, and there has been in some quarters an impression that it is not to be published. The report, however, is now in the hands of the printers and will be issued before Easter. It is understood that the report will provide little comfort for those who hope for cheaper inland telegrams. In fact, the Committee is averse to any reduction in the cost, and is doubtful whether the service can ever be made self-supporting even with the present high charges.

Article from *The Times* newspaper on the day that the Franchise Bill, later to be the Franchise Act of 1928, was published.

Constance Georgine Markievicz, the first woman to be elected to the British House of Commons in December 1918.